# QUOTABLE QUOTES
# OF MWALIMU
# JULIUS K. NYERERE

## COLLECTED FROM SPEECHES AND WRITINGS

# QUOTABLE QUOTES OF MWALIMU JULIUS K. NYERERE

COLLECTED FROM SPEECHES AND WRITINGS

## CHRISTOPHER C. LIUNDI

MKUKI NA NYOTA
DAR – ES – SALAAM

PUBLISHED BY
Mkuki na Nyota Publishers Ltd
Nyerere Road, Quality Plaza Building
P. O. Box 4246
Dar es Salaam, Tanzania
www.mkukinanyota.com
publish@mkukinanyota.com

© Christopher C. Liundi, 2012

ISBN 978 9987 08 154 7

# CONTENTS

# DEDICATION

This book of Quotable Quotes from Mwalimu Julius Kambarage Nyerere's speeches and writings is dedicated to a Tanzanian of Dutch origin; the late Rev. Fr. Johannes Franken, the Founder of the Teachers' College in Morogoro, Tanzania, known also as Kigurunyembe Teachers' College.

The late Fr. Franken was a true patriot of Tanzania, and a good friend and admirer of Mwalimu J. K. Nyerere. May their souls rest in peace. Amen.

# ACKNOWLEDGEMENTS

Special acknowledgement goes to my family, who "spared" me the time and gave me the needed ambiance for the work. Alongside my family, Madame Anna Mwansasu played a pivotal role in typing the manuscript and making cross-references. Her experience as a Secretary of the late Mwalimu Nyerere gives the work extra honour.

I would like to thank Oxford University Press Tanzania Limited for the permission to reproduce material from the Mwalimu Nyerere books, Freedom and Unity/Uhuru na Umoja, Freedom and Socialism/Uhuru na Ujamaa and Freedom and Development/Uhuru na Maendeleo.

Cover photo courtesy of the Ministry of Information, Youth Culture and Sports, Tanzania (Maelezo).

Mkuki na Nyota Publishers deserve special commendation for their encouragement when I "whispered" to them my desire to come up with a book of Mwalimu's quotations.

Of course there were many others who in one way or another had a hand in the work of this book. To all of them, including you, the reader, I say "*Asante*" ("Thank you").

# INTRODUCTION

President Julius Kambarage Nyerere was the first President of the United Republic of Tanzania and the Founder of the Nation of Tanzania. He came to power through the ballot – a democratic process – in 1961, and remained in power till 1985 he voluntarily stepped down. He died on 14ᵗʰ October 1999.

Throughout his term of office as a Tanganyika African National Union (TANU) party founder and activist to the time he was President and thereafter, he gave hundreds of speeches. Some were written and others given off the cuff. The articles and speeches were written in both English and

Swahili and were published in the Freedom series, published by Oxford University Press. He wrote other books including his translations into Swahili of Shakespear's Julius Ceasar (*Julias Kaizari*) and the Merchant of Venice, (*Mabepari wa Venisi*), a number of other books; "Our Leadership and the Destiny of Tanzania" (*Uongozi Wetu na Hatma ya Tanzania*) and several booklets on TANU and CCM policies.

Mwalimu Nyerere's books in the Freedom series are important and of great significance to Tanzania's politics. **Freedom and Unity** (*Uhuru na Umoja*), which contains a selection of his writings and speeches from 1952–1965 was the first of the three books. It was published in 1966 and reprinted in 1967, 1969 and 1970 respectively.

The second, **Freedom and Socialism** (*Uhuru na Ujamaa*) was published in 1968 and contains a selection of his writings and speeches made between 1965 and 1967. The last of the three books, **Freedom and Development** (*Uhuru na Maendeleo*), contains his speeches and writings between 1968 and 1973. Mwalimu's speeches and writings after 1973 were assembled by Mwalimu Nyerere Foundation and published in November 2011 by Oxford University Press.

The Mwalimu Nyerere Foundation (MNF) is a not – for profit making organization founded by Mwalimu Nyerere himself in 1996 and is dedicated to peace, unity, cooperation and development in Tanzania and beyond.

Mwalimu Nyerere was a very gifted and morally upright man. He was a true son of Africa- a Pan-Africanist, a nationalist, charismatic, a great orator, thinker, diplomat and above all a teacher. He humbly chose to be called simply '*Mwalimu*' – 'Teacher'.

To produce this small pocket book containing his many wise words is in a way to belittle his colossal contribution. He deserves a much bigger book of quotations.

The quotations in the Book are only those picked from the Freedom Series books, and his University Lectures. The quotations are arranged under the following themes:

Philosophy of Life, Equality of Man, Colonialism, Tanzania's Revolution, Democracy, Self-reliance, Rural Development, Non-Alignment, African Unity, the United Nations, Leadership and Education.

To conclude my introduction here is a quotation from Mwalimu which stressed the importance and pleasure of reading. He said:

"Books can break down the isolation of our lives and provide us with a friend wherever we may be."

This Book of Mwalimu's Quotable Quotes plays the role subscribed by Mwalimu Nyerere himself. It will be a good companion.

To benefit quickly from the quotations one should note they are thematically arranged to turn the light on the political development of Tanzania from colonialism to independence and beyond. All quotes, which express or fall under one theme are grouped together irrespective of the source of the book. Under each quotation, the page number is cited so that it can be traced to its source book. This is to facilitate finding the orginal quote so that it may be read in its original context.

*Christopher C. Liundi*

# 1

# ON PHILOSOPHY

"We have a number of different principles guiding our actions, and a number of different objectives: sometimes these principles and objectives clash."

FREEDOM AND UNITY: 6

"Group wealth and group power are not themselves virtues for which men would sacrifice themselves or for which they should be sacrificed. They are virtues only in so far as they serve the object of society– which is man."

FREEDOM AND UNITY: 7

"The principles of the traditional African family all the time encourage men to think of themselves as members of a society."

FREEDOM AND UNITY: 10

"Social principles are, by definition, ideals at which to strive and by which to exercise self-criticism. The question to ask is not whether they are capable of achievement, which is absurd, but whether a society of free men can do without them."

FREEDOM AND UNITY: 13

"The purpose of the society is man; but in order to serve man, there must be a social organization of economic activities which is conducive to the greater production of things useful for the material and spiritual welfare of man."

FREEDOM AND UNITY: 15

"Why then would it be a loss of freedom to refuse to allow attacks on the basic equality of all members of society or on the implications of that equality?"

FREEDOM AND UNITY: 15

"The question 'What profit would I myself get?' must be socially discouraged; it must be replaced by the question 'What benefit, and what loss, will be obtained by the people who make up this society?"

FREEDOM AND UNITY: 16

"We have to work towards a position where each person realizes that his rights in society-above the basic needs of every human being- must come second to the over-riding need of human dignity for all; and we have to establish the kind of social organization which reduces personal temptations above that level to a minimum."

FREEDOM AND UNITY: 17

"The only certain thing is that if we forget any of our principles, even when we are ignoring or breaking them, then we shall have betrayed the purpose of our revolution and Africa will fail to make its proper contribution to the development of mankind."

FREEDOM AND UNITY: 22

"We and our grandfathers and great grandfathers, have learned and adapted from nature, from ourselves, and from the people of Europe, America, and Asia. This we shall continue to do, just as men and civilization throughout the world have always done."

FREEDOM AND UNITY: 116

"Society like everything else must either move or stagnate– and in stagnation lies death. A mind unused atrophies and man without mind is nothing."

FREEDOM AND UNITY: 120

"If we are to make such a contribution to man's progress, then the most important thing for us to do now is to guard our freedom and to THINK as well as to act."

FREEDOM AND UNITY: 121

"A man stops himself from thinking if he assumes that anyone exists who cannot teach him something. He does so by accepting slogans or catchwords as revealing divine truths."

FREEDOM AND UNITY: 121

"The intellectual freedom of man, without which progress cannot take place, is confined by the prison wall of dogmatism."

FREEDOM AND UNITY: 121

"No one else can stop a man thinking, but he can stop himself, and indeed the temptation to do so is strong because thinking is hard work and introduces into life uncertainties only the strong can face."

FREEDOM AND UNITY: 121

"That slogans have their uses, I would be the last to deny, but they are valuable as reminders, as rallying calls. Like many other good things they are poisonous if taken to excess!"

FREEDOM AND UNITY: 121-122

Re: the non-conformist: "He it is who by the irritation he causes, stops society from ceasing to think, forces it to make constant re-evaluations and adjustments."

FREEDOM AND UNITY: 122

"If you break a principle, it will find a method of breaking you. And if a people try to break a major principle, those principles find a way of breaking that people."

FREEDOM AND UNITY: 127

"We in Africa are now ONE, and we must remain so."

FREEDOM AND UNITY: 161

"Socialism, like democracy, is an attitude of mind. In socialist society it is the socialist attitude of mind, and not the rigid adherence to a standard political pattern, which is needed to ensure that the people care for each other's welfare."

FREEDOM AND UNITY: 162

"But the man who uses the wealth for the purpose of dominating any of his fellows is a capitalist."

FREEDOM AND UNITY: 162

"African socialism: It has nothing to do with the possession or non-possession of wealth."

FREEDOM AND UNITY: 162

"...a millionaire can be a good socialist. But a socialist millionaire is a rare phenomenon."

FREEDOM AND UNITY: 162

"For it is not efficiency of production nor the amount of wealth in a country, which makes millionaires; it is the uneven distribution of what is produced."

FREEDOM AND UNITY: 162

"There must be something wrong in a society where one man, however hard– working or clever he may be, can acquire as great a 'reward' as a thousand of his fellows can acquire between them."

FREEDOM AND UNITY: 163

"... a millionaire could be a socialist. But he could hardly be the product of a socialist society."

FREEDOM AND UNITY: 163

"Acquisitiveness for the purpose of gaining power and prestige is unsocialist."

FREEDOM AND UNITY: 163

"Not only was the capitalist, or the landed exploiter unknown to traditional African society, but we did not have that other form of modern parasite– the loiterer, or idler, who accepts the hospitality of society as his 'right' but gives nothing in return."

FREEDOM AND UNITY: 165

"There is no such thing as socialism without work."

FREEDOM AND UNITY: 165

"We must, as I have said... regain our former attitude of mind–our traditional African socialism–and apply it to the new societies we are building today."

FREEDOM AND UNITY: 167

"We cannot hope to solve our problems by pretending they do not exist."

FREEDOM AND UNITY: 179

"Those of you who have capital or who own property, do not try to use your wealth as a weapon with which to oppress your brothers."

FREEDOM AND UNITY: 182

"I would like to see that wherever two or three of us meet, even if it is in a bar, or on a bus, or at school, or at the market, or the *shamba* or in the office, in a shop or outside in the open, that place becomes a classroom for discussing and learning about Ujamaa and about the two main instruments of Ujamaa, the Government and the Cooperative Movement."

FREEDOM AND UNITY: 185

"Ujamaa is a way of life, and there are no experts better qualified than yourself to expound that way of life. We are all of us Ujamaa experts."

FREEDOM AND UNITY: 186

"...I would like to see every single one of us a teacher and an instrument of Ujamaa."

FREEDOM AND UNITY: 185

"And once you deal in dogma you cannot allow freedom of opinion. You cannot have dogma without putting contrary ideas on the 'Index.'"

FREEDOM AND UNITY: 201

"The leadership of our movement is instantly changing; there is no reason why the leadership of the nation should not also be changing."

FREEDOM AND UNITY: 201

"One of the basic purposes of the independence struggle is to get the right to think for ourselves and apply the results of our thinking."

FREEDOM AND UNITY: 207

"Even between socialist countries the class divisions are getting greater. There are now not only rich capitalist countries and poor capitalist countries. There are also rich socialist countries and poor socialist countries. Further, I believe that the socialist countries themselves, considered as 'individuals' in the larger society of nations, are now committing the same crime as was committed by the capitalists before. On the international level they are now beginning to use wealth for capitalist purposes that is, for the acquisition of power and prestige."

FREEDOM AND UNITY: 208

"This is the coming division of the world– a class, not an ideological division. And unless we begin to act now in accordance with our declared socialist convictions, we shall find that it is a division with capitalist and socialist countries on both sides of the conflict."

FREEDOM AND UNITY: 208

"We are committed to a philosophy of African Socialism, and basic to this is the principle of human equality. One of our concerns therefore, must be to prevent the growth of a class structure in our society..."

FREEDOM AND UNITY: 210-

"A true revolutionary is not an unrealistic dreamer. A true revolutionary is the one who analyses any given situation with scientific objectivity and then acts accordingly."

FREEDOM AND UNITY: 217

"We must, and do, demand that this University takes an active part in the social revolution we are engineering."

FREEDOM AND UNITY: 219

"... for prejudices are the point to which men retreat when the real problems are tough and when they are not prepared to face the implications of their personal or community difficulties."

FREEDOM AND UNITY: 219

"I refer to the most prevalent social disease of the twentieth century– discrimination on grounds of race, colour or caste."

FREEDOM AND UNITY: 219

"The basis of human progress throughout history has been the existence of people who, regardless of the consequences to themselves, stood up when they believed it necessary, and said 'That is wrong; this is what we should do ...' If we know that the world is round we must say so, even if the majority of our people may still think that it is flat."

FREEDOM AND UNITY: 221

"Because I cannot claim that I, any more than my colleagues, will never mistake honest criticism for unconstitutional opposition."

FREEDOM AND UNITY: 221

"...we in Tanganyika would reject creation of a rural class system even if it could be proved that this gives the largest overall production increase. We would reject this method of securing national economic improvement because it would defeat the total purpose of change, which is the well–being of all our people."

FREEDOM AND UNITY: 237

"Living in a community gives man an enlarged opportunity to improve his well–being and develop himself to the full; only by cooperating with his fellows can man really live in maximum freedom. Yet at the same time, it is life with his fellows which restricts his freedom. He can no longer do exactly what he wishes, when he wishes to do it."

FREEDOM AND UNITY: 267

"Cooperation and conflict are two sides of the same coin; both arise out of man's relationship with his fellows. The larger the group, the greater the possibility of development through cooperation, and the greater the possibility of conflict."

FREEDOM AND UNITY: 267

"But revolutions do not just happen– least of all economic revolutions; they demand scientific and objective thought, and the reasoned application of basic principles of the existing situation, and the deliberate conversion of unpleasant facts into something more palatable."

FREEDOM AND UNITY: 308

"Facts– whether they be political, economic or social– have to be recognized and used or circumvented if this latter course is possible. They cannot be ignored. Very often facts are extremely unpleasant and it is more comfortable to close your eyes and pretend they are not there, or like Don Quixote, to impose a private dream world on the realities with which we are surrounded."

FREEDOM AND UNITY: 308

"There is no short cut, no easy solution which can be applied to the problems of developing our country. Slogans will not give our people more to eat; and nor will blaming our failures on any other country or on any other group of our own people."

FREEDOM AND UNITY: 308


"Don Quixote could rescue maidens from non–existent dragons; he could mentally convert dilapidated farmhouses into romantic castles, and no harm was done to anyone except himself. But if we in the United Republic try to indulge in a similar kind of romanticism then the political revolution we have carried out and the economic revolution we are now beginning will both collapse in misery."

FREEDOM AND UNITY: 309


"Only careful thought about our own problems and the relentless application of scientific and objective thinking can enable us to achieve the betterment of our lives to which we are committed."

FREEDOM AND UNITY: 309

"Only when we are clear what we are trying to do can we begin to think about the way of doing it."

FREEDOM AND UNITY: 310

"The people and the government of the United Republic are aiming to build a just society of free and equal citizens, who live in healthy conditions, who control their own destiny, and who cooperate together and with other people in a spirit of human brotherhood for mutual benefit. This is the goal. It is certainly not a description of our present society ..."

FREEDOM AND UNITY: 311

"We all accept that every child should have the right to attend school, and to develop his mind to its maximum capacity. Yet that does not solve the problem of what we do now, when our resources are insufficient for both universal primary education and a system of secondary schools and university education. Only clear thinking about the priorities of educational advance in the light of our other goals, can lead to a decision on such matters as these."

FREEDOM AND UNITY: 311

"Even where basic principles are clearly involved, the need for a rational approach remains. Because usually more than one principle is involved, and they often conflict."

FREEDOM AND UNITY: 311

"While the vast mass of the people give full and active support to this country and its government, a handful of individuals can still put our nation into jeopardy, and reduce to ashes the efforts of millions."

FREEDOM AND UNITY: 312

"Here, in this Union conditions may well arise in which it is better that ninety–nine innocent people should suffer temporary detention than that one possible traitor should wreck the nation. It would certainly be complete madness to let ninety–nine guilty men escape in order to avoid the risk of punishing one innocent person. Our ideals must guide us, not blind us."

FREEDOM AND UNITY: 313

"For it is comparatively easy to build a nation of well-fed robots who have no ideas of their own, or to have a society where everyone can talk while they are starving."
FREEDOM AND UNITY: 313

"There is never a single 'correct' answer when a conflict of principles is concerned."
FREEDOM AND UNITY: 313

"This essential scientific thinking cannot be left to the President and his colleagues in the government. Every educated person must take part, and the University College of Dar es Salaam, its staff and its students, have a vital role to play– now and in the future..."
FREEDOM AND UNITY: 315

"Hard thought and detailed negotiations have now to replace slogans if the objective is to be attained."
FREEDOM AND UNITY: 334

"Tanzania is not now a socialist country; it is only a country whose people have firmly committed themselves to building socialism."
FREEDOM AND SOCIALISM: 1

"For socialism is not built by Government decisions, nor by Acts of Parliament; a country does not become socialist by nationalizations or grand designs on paper. It is more difficult than that to build socialism, and it takes much longer."

FREEDOM AND SOCIALISM: 2

"By the use of the world *'ujamaa'*, therefore, we state that for us socialism involves building on the foundation of our past, and building also to our own design. We are not importing a foreign ideology into Tanzania and trying to smother our distinct social patterns with it."

FREEDOM AND SOCIALISM: 2

"It would be absurd to suggest that because differences will exist between different socialist societies in different parts of the world, that therefore 'socialism' has no meaning, or that it is too vague a concept to be sensibly adopted as the social goal of a young country."

FREEDOM AND SOCIALISM: 3

"The word 'man' to a socialist, means all men– all human beings. Male and female; black, white, brown, yellow; long–nosed and short–nosed..."

FREEDOM AND SOCIALISM: 4

"A man who cheats his fellows by dishonesty, who fails to do a full day's work, or who fails to co–operate with his fellows because he wants to bolster his own personal interests, is exploiting other men."

FREEDOM AND SOCIALISM: 7

"The fact that socialism and religion are two different things does not mean that socialism is anti–religious."

FREEDOM AND SOCIALISM: 13

"This necessity for religious toleration arises out of the nature of socialism. For a man's religious beliefs are important to him, and the purpose of socialism is Man."

FREEDOM AND SOCIALISM: 13

"There is, however, an apparent tendency among certain socialists to try and establish a new religion– a religion of socialism itself."

FREEDOM AND SOCIALISM: 14

"This attempt to create a new religion out of socialism is absurd. It is not scientific, and it is almost certainly not Marxist– for however combatant and quarrelsome a socialist Marx was, he never claimed to be an infallible divinity!"

FREEDOM AND SOCIALISM: 15

"Speaking generally, and despite the existence of a few feudalistic communities, traditional Tanzanian society had many socialist characteristics."

FREEDOM AND SOCIALISM: 16

"Despite the low level of material progress, traditional African society was in practice organized on a basis which was in accordance with socialist principles."

FREEDOM AND SOCIALISM: 16

"Nor would it be very scientific to reject Africa's past when trying to build socialism in Africa."

FREEDOM AND SOCIALISM: 16

"Socialism is about people, and people are the products of their history, education and environment. It is absurd to assume that while democracy has to be adopted to the circumstances of the country in order that the people's will shall be effective, socialism can just be copied from somewhere else."

FREEDOM AND SOCIALISM: 20

"They are saying that the perfect answer to the problems of man in society is already known, and all we have to do is to copy others. Once again, they are saying that Africa has nothing to contribute to the world and all good things come from elsewhere. And then, in their insecurity, they look for a 'certificate of socialist approval' from the country or party which they believe has these answers."

FREEDOM AND SOCIALISM: 20-21

"The word *ujamaa* denotes the kind of life lived by a man and his family– father, mother, children and near relatives."

FREEDOM AND SOCIALISM: 137

"A university which tries to put its professors and its students into blinkers will neither serve the cause of knowledge, nor the interests of the society in which it exists."

FREEDOM AND SOCIALISM: 182

"...when we say that Tanzania is aiming at building 'African Socialism' we mean that we intend to adopt the same attitude in the new circumstances of a nation state which is increasingly using modern techniques of economic production."

FREEDOM AND SOCIALISM: 199

"Socialism is a way of life, and a socialist society cannot simply come into existence. A socialist society can only be built by those who believe in, and who themselves practice, the principles of socialism."

FREEDOM AND SOCIALISM: 234

"Traditional African society was not called 'socialist', it was just life. Yet it was socialist in the principles upon which it was based."

FREEDOM AND SOCIALISM: 312

"The Arusha Declaration is a declaration of intent; no more than that. It states the goals towards which TANU will be leading the people of Tanzania, and it indicates the direction of development."

UNIVERSITY LECTURE: 5TH AUGUST 1967

"This growth must come out of our own roots, not through the grafting on to those roots of something which is alien to them. This is very important, for it means that we cannot adopt any political 'holy book' and try to implement its rulings– with or without revision."

UNIVERSITY LECTURE: 5TH AUGUST 1967

"The real question, therefore, is whether each of us is prepared to accept the challenge of building a state in which no man is ashamed of his poverty in the light of another's affluence, and no man has to be ashamed of his affluence in the light of another's poverty."

UNIVERSITY LECTURE: 5TH AUGUST 1967

"Our object must be to develop in such a manner as to ensure that the advantages of modern knowledge and modern methods are achieved, but without the spread of capitalism."

MBIONI VOL. IV NO. III

"But because we are seeking to grow from our own roots and to preserve that which is valuable in our traditional past, we have also to stop thinking in terms of massive agricultural mechanization and the proletarianization of our rural population."

MBIONI: VOL. IV NO. III P. 8

"But, most of all, we have to reactivate the philosophy of cooperation in production and sharing in distribution which was an essential part of traditional African Society."

MBIONI: VOL. IV NO. III P 15

"...freedom... it has to be won, and protected, by those who desire it."

FREEDOM AND DEVELOPMENT: 3

"The community must own, control, and run its own activities."

FREEDOM AND DEVELOPMENT: 6

"One thing is certainly known; nothing succeeds like success!"

FREEDOM AND DEVELOPMENT: 6

"If the doctor orders certain treatment for the patient, it must be carried out by the nurse without argument, and without carelessness... the hospital discipline must be maintained or the person must accept dismissal."

FREEDOM AND DEVELOPMENT: 64

"Our peasants are very much behind in modern development. Our policies demand that we speed up the development plans for the rural areas..."

FREEDOM AND DEVELOPMENT: 155

# 2

# ON DEMOCRACY

## SECTION A: EQUALITY

"Wherever extreme poverty exists beside a visibly high standard of living, there is the risk of bitterness..."

FREEDOM AND UNITY: 73

"Let not the world point a finger at us and say that we gained our freedom on a moral argument– the argument of the brotherhood of man– and then threw that argument overboard, and began ourselves to discriminate against our brothers on the grounds of colour; I pray, sir, that Almighty God will save us from committing such a sin against His justice."

FREEDOM AND UNITY: 79

"The division of any society into the 'haves'
and 'have-nots' is... dynamite."
FREEDOM AND UNITY: 80

"A united Africa does not mean a uniform
Africa."
FREEDOM AND UNITY: 117

"Discrimination against human beings
because of their colour, is exactly what we
have been fighting against."
FREEDOM AND UNITY: 128

"If we are going to base citizenship on colour,
we will commit a crime."
FREEDOM AND UNITY: 128

"...use it (political power) to build a
Tanganyika in which there will not be so
much as one individual citizen who is made
to feel that he is a second rate citizen."
FREEDOM AND UNITY: 182

"The only distinction which can in future be
accepted is that between citizens and non-
citizens..."
FREEDOM AND UNITY: 259

"Here in East Africa, for the sake of the majority as much as that of any minority, we have to guard against the prejudice which would simply reverse the racial positions existing in South Africa."

FREEDOM AND UNITY: 219

"Racialism is based on the same assumption, that one man has the right to determine the limits of freedom for another simply because the latter is physically different in appearance."

FREEDOM AND UNITY: 227

"And if I am humiliated merely for existing, then I have no alternative but to fight, with whatever weapons are available. Yet this sort of fighting prevents us all, the man who discriminates as well as me, from living a full life, or contributing to human progress."

FREEDOM AND UNITY: 228

"But it would be quite wrong for us to continue to discriminate between Tanganyika citizens on any grounds other than those of character, and ability to do specific tasks. We cannot allow the growth of first and second class citizenship. Each Tanganyika citizen must accept all the duties, and receive all the rights, which our citizenship implies. All must be governed by the same laws, must receive the same respect from his fellow, and have the same opportunities to earn a living and to serve the nation of which he is a member. Anything other than this would now mean intolerable hypocrisy. The distinction between citizens of African descent and citizens of non–African descent must now be ended."

FREEDOM AND UNITY: 259


"And it would be a double humiliation for us to discriminate against Tanganyika citizens who are able and willing to serve their country and at the same time to beg non–citizens to come and work for us."

FREEDOM AND UNITY: 260

"Everywhere in the world there are people who suffer from the disease of believing themselves to be inherently superior to those of another colour or another race – we have these people in Tanzania too. But only in South Africa is this disease deliberately propagated and forced into the social structure."

FREEDOM AND UNITY: 330

"The equality of man may or may not be susceptible to scientific proof. But its acceptance as a basic assumption of life in the society is the core and essence of socialism."

FREEDOM AND SOCIALISM: 4

"...racialism is absolutely and fundamentally contrary to the first principle of socialism– the equality of man."

FREEDOM AND SOCIALISM: 30

"A citizen of this country is a citizen: that is enough. Let us never forget that fact, and let no one of us ever again betray the people by acting as if there were different classes of citizens."

FREEDOM AND SOCIALISM: 92

"But, the man or woman who hates 'Jews,' or 'Asians,' 'Europeans,' or even 'West Europeans and Americans' is not a socialist."

FREEDOM AND SOCIALISM: 258

"To try and divide up the people working for our nation into groups of 'good' and 'bad' according to their skin colour, or their national origin, or their tribal origin, is to sabotage the work we have just embarked upon."

FREEDOM AND SOCIALISM: 260

"...each one of us must fight, in himself, the racialist habits of thought which were part of our inheritance from colonialism."

FREEDOM AND SOCIALISM: 261

"We have dedicated ourselves to build a socialist society in Tanzania. And, socialism and racialism are incompatible."

FREEDOM AND SOCIALISM: 261

"Yet socialism is not Utopian. Nor is it unaware that men are unequal in their capacities. On the contrary, it is based on the facts of human nature. It is a doctrine which accepts mankind as it is, and demands such an organization of society that man's inequalities are put to the service of his equality."

FREEDOM AND SOCIALISM: 303

"The person who claims to use the Arusha Declaration in support of attacks on any particular racial community, is betraying both his ignorance and his rejection of the principles enunciated in it."

UNIVERSITY LECTURE: 5/5/1967

"...it is impossible for one people to free another people, or even to defend the freedom of another people."

FREEDOM AND DEVELOPMENT: 3

"It is that as we, the peoples of the earth, extend human justice so we are furthering the cause of peace; and that every moment of peace is a moment stolen unless it is used to further justice between men and between nations."

FREEDOM AND DEVELOPMENT: 4

"...negotiations are not always easy. They demand a willingness to compromise on the part of all participants; an understanding of what is essential, and an acceptance of the fact that no one country can hope to get everything it wants."

FREEDOM AND DEVELOPMENT: 21

"I admit that in the modern world real friendship between very big nations and very small nations is a comparatively rare thing."

FREEDOM AND DEVELOPMENT: 40

"Socialism is good, in other words, because it is people–centred... And service of the people means, at its very lowest, that all shall have sufficient food, clothing and shelter..."

FREEDOM AND DEVELOPMENT: 46

"To poor people, what is called 'cost effectiveness' is absolutely vital... For, I repeat: to plan is to choose."

FREEDOM AND DEVELOPMENT: 101

"...the Union between Tanganyika and Zanzibar is a demonstration that unity can be achieved if the will exists, in spite of the difficulties."

FREEDOM AND DEVELOPMENT: 177

"There is a world-wide movement now even within the imperialist countries it exists – to put an end to the exploitation of man by man."

FREEDOM AND DEVELOPMENT: 371

"If a country expects other people to respect its passports, then it must itself respect them. Citizenship must be respected without discrimination, or it will be met with disrespect without discrimination."

FREEDOM AND DEVELOPMENT: 372

## SECTION B: COLONIALISM

"Years of Arab slave raiding, and later years of European domination, had caused our people to have grave doubts about their own abilities. This was no accident; any dominating group seeks to destroy the confidence of those they dominate because this helps them to maintain their position, and the oppressors in Tanganyika were no exception."

FREEDOM AND UNITY: 3

"A vital task for any liberation movement must therefore be to restore the people's self–confidence..."

FREEDOM AND UNITY: 3

"The African's capacity for bearing insult is not really limitless."

FREEDOM AND UNITY: 28

"...how easy it is to inflame an insulted people."

FREEDOM AND UNITY: 28

"A day comes when the people will prefer death to insult and woe to the people who will see that day!"

FREEDOM AND UNITY: 28

"I love a fight, but it is no use fighting the wrong enemy or fighting an imaginary enemy."
FREEDOM AND UNITY: 101

"Do not waste time in fighting battles that are over, in belabouring enemies who are already dead. Neither Africa nor the world is going to judge us by the amount of venom we pour against the old or even the new form of colonialism."
FREEDOM AND UNITY: 115

"...domination is no less domination– though it may be physically less painful– because it wears a kid glove."
FREEDOM AND UNITY: 133

"Our whole existence has been controlled by people with an alien attitude to life, people with different customs and beliefs."
FREEDOM AND UNITY: 133

"I want to assure... that we in Tanganyika are prepared to die a little for the final removal of the humiliation of colonialism from the face of Africa..."
FREEDOM AND UNITY: 216 – 217

"For too long we in this country have s
uffered from the results of a colonial attitude
of mind – and one which unfortunately did
not depart with the colonial government."
FREEDOM AND UNITY: 316

"For too long we in Africa– and Tanzania as
part of Africa – have slept, and allowed the
rest of the world to walk round and over us."
FREEDOM AND SOCIALISM: 32

"...the enemy we have to fight does not kill
us with bullets, but weakens us with disease,
tempts us to slothfulness, and encourages us
to indulge in the boastfulness of conspicuous
consumption when all our energies are needed
for the work ahead."
FREEDOM AND SOCIALISM: 34

"For years we have been reminding the
world that one third of Africa does not have
independence or democracy. I cannot honestly
claim that this fact seems to worry the Western
press or the Western politicians very much. I
can assure you that it worries us."
FREEDOM AND SOCIALISM: 52

"The struggle has to continue until final victory; colonialism must be wiped out in Africa before any post-colonial independent state can feel secure."

FREEDOM AND SOCIALISM: 144

"...talk of a non-aggression treaty between South Africa and Tanzania is such nonsense... The conflict is about apartheid versus humanity, and about our right to freedom."

FREEDOM AND DEVELOPMENT 209

"...racialism is itself an aggression against the human spirit, as colonialism is the result of a past aggression against a people and a territory."

FREEDOM AND DEVELOPMENT 209

## SECTION C: DEMOCRACY

"...aristocracy is something foreign to Africa."

**FREEDOM AND UNITY: 103**

"Traditionally the African knows no class."

**FREEDOM AND UNITY: 103**

"The traditional Africans society, whether it had a chief or not... was a society of equals and it conducted its business through discussion."

**FREEDOM AND UNITY: 103**

"...these three then I consider to be essential to democratic government: discussion, equality, and freedom– the last being implied by the other two."

**FREEDOM AND UNITY: 103**

"It was possible for the ancient Greeks to boast of 'democracy' when more than half the population had no say at all in the conduct of the affairs of the State."

**FREEDOM AND UNITY: 104**

"...it was possible for Abraham Lincoln to bequeath to us a perfect definition of democracy although he spoke in a slave-owning society."

FREEDOM AND UNITY: 109

"...it was possible for friends the British to brag about 'democracy' and still build a great Empire for the glory of the Britons."

FREEDOM AND UNITY: 104

"...the African's mental concept of 'Government' was personal– not institutional."

FREEDOM AND UNITY: 105

"When the word 'government' was mentioned, the African thought of the chief; he did not, as the Britons, think of a grand building in which a debate was taking place."

FREEDOM AND UNITY: 105

"An organized opposition is not an essential element, although a society which has no room and no time for the harmless eccentric can hardly be called 'democratic.'"

FREEDOM AND UNITY: 106

"If... you have a two-party system where the difference between the parties are not fundamental, then you immediately reduce politics to the level of a football match."
FREEDOM AND UNITY: 196–197

"No party which limits its membership to a clique can ever free itself from fear of overthrow by those it has excluded."
FREEDOM AND UNITY: 201

"Democracy is another essential characteristic of a socialist society. For the people's equality must be reflected in the political organization; everyone must be an equal participant in the government of his society."
FREEDOM AND SOCIALISM: 5

"But elections are not the beginning and end of democracy."
FREEDOM AND SOCIALISM: 5

"Success in a socialist society will imply that a man has earned the respect, admiration, and love of his fellow citizens, by his desire to serve, and by the contribution he has made to the well-being of the community."
FREEDOM AND SOCIALISM: 9

"...when you are discussing difficulties or failures, I hope that you will be prepared to go to the root of the matter, if necessary."

FREEDOM AND SOCIALISM: 111

"It would thus be a gross misinterpretation of our needs to suggest that the educational system should be designed to produce robots, who work hard but never question what the leaders in government or TANU are doing and saying."

FREEDOM AND SOCIALISM: 274

"...there neither is, nor will be, a political 'holy book' which purports to give all the answers to all the social, political and economic problems which will face our country in the future."

FREEDOM AND SOCIALISM: 274

"But the educational system of Tanzania would not be serving the interests of a democratic socialist society if it tried to stop people from thinking about the teachings, policies or the beliefs of leaders, either past or present. Only free people conscious of their worth and their equality can build a free society."

FREEDOM AND SOCIALISM: 275

"For words without actions simply lay us open to ridicule. Unfortunately it is those who do not intend to follow their words with actions who usually shout the loudest."

FREEDOM AND SOCIALISM: 299

"It is imperative that socialists continue thinking. And this thinking must be more than an attempt to discover what any so-called socialist Bible or socialist Koran really says and means."

FREEDOM AND SOCIALISM: 302

## SECTION D: ON LEADERSHIP

"I believe myself corruption in a country should be treated in almost the same way as you treat treason."
FREEDOM AND UNITY: 82

"It would be both wrong, and certainly unnecessary, to feel we must wait until the leaders are dead before we begin to criticize them!"
FREEDOM AND UNITY: 202

"We must begin to treat pomposity with the scorn it deserves. Dignity does not need pomposity to uphold it."
FREEDOM AND UNITY: 226

"One of the most difficult things to secure from a government composed of different Ministries is a coordinated and cooperative attack on a particular problem. Each Ministry or department seems to regard the others as its rivals to be appeased or called upon when this is inevitable, but generally to be ignored."
FREEDOM AND UNITY: 237

"When only the law of the jungle reigns, the struggle for existence must naturally end up with survival of the fittest. This may be alright when it applies to beasts; as a method of contact between human beings it is intolerable."

FREEDOM AND UNITY: 247

"But the peace resulting from imposed law is short-lived. The moment a man feels himself strong enough he tries to throw off this law and substitute another more to his liking."

FREEDOM AND UNITY: 268

"The only system of law which brings stable peace is a system which is based on the fundamental human equality of all the people under its suzerainty, and which aims at reconciling to the greatest possible degree man's conflicting desires for individual freedom and the benefits of communal life."

FREEDOM AND UNITY: 268

"...law which cannot be enforced is liable to deteriorate into an expression of pious hopes."

FREEDOM AND UNITY: 269

"...until we were colonized this 'nation' did not exist, different laws operated among the constituent tribes and there was conflict between them. It was the colonial power which imposed a common law and maintained it by force, until the growth of the independence movement put the flesh of an emotional unity on to the skeleton of legal unity."

FREEDOM AND UNITY: 271

"Law which offends against basic human rights, or which fails to secure those rights, does not fulfill the purpose of law, because it does not secure man's life in society."

FREEDOM AND UNITY: 282

"Under these circumstances responsibility cannot be entrusted to people for sentimental reasons, or left with them once they have failed just because they are nice people. Neither are these the circumstances under which it is sensible to worry about the skin colour or religion of those who are involved in the work of getting the bus to move forward and upward."

FREEDOM AND UNITY: 309

"The senior posts of our public service cannot be used as if they were rewards for past effort. They must be filled by those who can now make the particular contribution to our national effort that the job in question calls for."

FREEDOM AND UNITY: 310

"We have always to remember that our people did not fight for independence from the British in order to install a local tyranny."

FREEDOM AND UNITY: 313

"Such reports in fact, leave certain things out of account; in particular, they do not determine how we shall react to the facts they present."

FREEDOM AND UNITY: 320

"It is true that for some jobs to be done effectively certain extra facilities are needed by the workers; a teacher or an administrator, for example, will need a place where he can study quietly, will need to be able to obtain books of a certain type, and so on. But does anyone need a palace while another receives only 'bed space'?"

FREEDOM AND SOCIALISM: 6-7

"The Rule of Law is a part of socialism; until it prevails socialism does not prevail. By itself the Rule of Law does not bring socialism; but you cannot have socialism without it, because it is the expression of man's equality in one facet of social living."

**FREEDOM AND SOCIALISM: 8**

"Socialist leadership is of the people; it cannot be imposed by force or tyranny."

**FREEDOM AND SOCIALISM: 24**

"For to build socialism you must have socialists – particularly in leading positions."

**FREEDOM AND SOCIALISM: 26**

"The only way in which leadership can be maintained as a people's leadership is if the leaders have reason to fear the judgment of the people."

**FREEDOM AND SOCIALISM: 26**

"...the people are ready and anxious for change – they only need leadership based on human respect."

**FREEDOM AND SOCIALISM: 31**

"We refuse to put ourselves in a strait-jacket of constitutional devices— even of our own making. The constitution of Tanzania must serve the people of Tanzania. We do not intend that the people of Tanzania should serve the constitution."

FREEDOM AND SOCIALISM: 37

"...elections are not a vote of thanks. It would be quite wrong to elect a person to Parliament because in the past they have done good work. The elections choose people for the future."

FREEDOM AND SOCIALISM: 90

"...there is no personal security for Members of parliament, for members of the Government, or even for the President. Politics is, and must be looked upon as afield of service, not as a means of earning a living."

FREEDOM AND SOCIALISM: 90

"If our Party drifts into becoming an elitist organization, with special privileges for founder members or others, then democracy in Tanzania will die."

FREEDOM AND SOCIALISM: 91

"Members of Parliament are not delegates; they are representatives."
FREEDOM AND SOCIALISM: 95

"Fulfilling the wishes of the people does not always mean taking the most popular course."
FREEDOM AND SOCIALISM: 95

"...in accordance with my duties under the constitution, I shall insist that corruption in any form is exposed to the gaze of the people."
FREEDOM AND SOCIALISM: 95

"The farmers– the mass of the people of our country– will not change their traditional methods because someone with a diploma comes and tells them that change is good."
FREEDOM AND SOCIALISM: 105

"It is impossible for the judiciary to continue to operate in the colonial tradition when everything else in the society is changing."
FREEDOM AND SOCIALISM: 109

"It is easy to call on others for sacrifice."
FREEDOM AND SOCIALISM: 129

"Land was the property of all the people, and those who used it did not do so because it was their property."
FREEDOM AND SOCIALISM: 137

"Our aim is to abolish this division of people between masters and servants, and to make every person a master– not a master who oppresses others, but one who serves himself."
FREEDOM AND SOCIALISM 139

"...this habit of evading responsibility has been inherited. We have been led to accept the division of men into masters and slaves."
FREEDOM AND SOCIALISM: 139

"We fear to take decisions. This is why some people tell me to decide things for them on the grounds that we know better."
FREEDOM AND SOCIALISM: 140

"I shall keep on urging Tanzanians not to fear their leaders."
FREEDOM AND SOCIALISM: 140

"When you are selected to lead your fellow men, it does not mean that you know everything better than they do."

FREEDOM AND SOCIALISM: 140

"When you have pushed a load a little way up a hill it is no use relaxing. You have to go on. Otherwise the load may well fall back to its original position– and perhaps crush the people in the process."

FREEDOM AND SOCIALISM: 169

"...none of us could, or should, assume that what we have decided to be right for ourselves must automatically be right for others."

FREEDOM AND DEVELOPMENT: 3

"...reject the proposition that intellectuals are a special breed of men and women... intellectuals have a special contribution to make to the development of our nations and to Africa."

FREEDOM AND DEVELOPMENT 28

"...the Party has also to ensure that the government stays in close touch with the feelings, the difficulties and the aspiration of the people."
FREEDOM AND DEVELOPMENT: 32


"...if anyone is unwilling to accept his responsibilities in this matter, then he must accept the penalties of his failure."
FREEDOM AND DEVELOPMENT: 65


"Anyone who refuses to accept a very obvious truth... and says that the reason is tribalism must provide us with the evidence for his statement."
FREEDOM AND DEVELOPMENT: 76


"Everyone of us, through improving his own education, can begin to make improvements in his own life..."
FREEDOM AND DEVELOPMENT 140

# 3

# ON EDUCATION

"If these principles are to be preserved and adapted to serve the larger societies which have now grown up, the whole of the new modern educational system must also be directed towards inculcating them. They must underlie all the things taught in the schools, all the things broadcasted in the radio, all the things written in the press. And if they are to form the basis which society operates, then no advocacy of opposition to these principles can be allowed."

FREEDOM AND UNITY: 14

"One cannot say that the educated are responsible for a smaller share of the miseries of mankind than the uneducated. History has not proved that..."

FREEDOM AND UNITY: 77

"The educated are not necessarily more honest, more patriotic, or more selfless than the uneducated... They are not necessarily more wise."

FREEDOM AND UNITY: 77

"The students will go as Africans seeking to learn how our needs can be helped by experience abroad; they will not have to learn the lessons first and then return to see whether what they have learned can be fitted into our needs."

FREEDOM AND UNITY: 131

"For while other people can aim at reaching the moon, and while in the future we might aim at reaching the moon, our present plans must be directed at reaching the villages."

FREEDOM AND UNITY: 131

"Our young men's ambition was not to become well-educated Africans, but to become Black Europeans."

FREEDOM AND UNITY: 186

"A nation which refuses to learn from foreign culture is nothing but a nation of idiots and lunatics... But to learn from other cultures does not mean we should abandon our own."

FREEDOM AND UNITY: 187

"Our actions are forming the traditions of the future; what we do and how we react to external events will set a pattern which our descendants may find difficult to break."

FREEDOM AND UNITY: 252

"...the organization and the teaching will emphasize man's co-operative spirit- his desire to work in harmony with his friends and neighbours- not his personal aggressiveness. Second, it will reserve its highest respect and its highest prizes for those whose life and work demonstrate the greatest service, not the greatest personal acquisitiveness."

FREEDOM AND SOCIALISM: 8-9

"It is necessary that we should realize that our young people out of school are not disqualified from being farmers. They are qualified to be better farmers, and better citizens."

FREEDOM AND SOCIALISM: 72

"The most effective classroom is an efficient farm. The most effective teachers are the efficient farmers."

FREEDOM AND SOCIALISM: 105

"An agriculturalist should not be a man with clean, soft hands. He must be a practical man, who uses his hands at the same time as he uses his head."

FREEDOM AND SOCIALISM: 105

"Sometimes my own mother calls me and gives me some advice. She tells me not to do this or that. She advises me even in matters of government."

FREEDOM AND SOCIALISM: 140

"Does it mean that a person who does not have formal education is a fool? What does education mean? An uneducated man has a brain– given to him by God. Does a man become a goat because he is uneducated?"

FREEDOM AND SOCIALISM: 140

"What we expect from our university is both a complete objectivity in the search for truth, and also commitment to our society–a desire to serve it. We expect the two things equally. And I do not believe this dual responsibility–to objectivity and to service– is impossible of fulfillment."

FREEDOM AND SOCIALISM: 182

"We tax the people to build these places only so that young men and women may become efficient servants to them. There is no other justification for this heavy call being made on poor peasants."

FREEDOM AND SOCIALISM: 184

"...certainly as a body there is always a temptation for students to regard themselves as a group which has rights without responsibilities."

FREEDOM AND SOCIALISM: 185

"The education provided must therefore encourage the development in each citizen of three things; an enquiring mind; and ability to learn from what others do, and reject or adapt it to his own needs; and a basic confidence in his own position as a free and equal member of the society, who values others and is valued by them for what he does and not for what he obtains."

FREEDOM AND SOCIALISM: 274

"...a man is not necessarily wise because he is old; a man cannot necessarily run a factory because he has been working in it as a labourer or store-keeper for 20 years. But equally he may not be able to do so if he has a Doctorate in Commerce."

FREEDOM AND SOCIALISM: 277

"We cannot integrate the pupils and students into the future society simply by theoretical teaching, however well designed it is."

NOT FOUNDFREEDOM AND SOCIALISM: 281


"Further education for a selected few must be education for service to the many. There can be no other justification for taxing the many to give education to only a few."

FREEDOM AND SOCIALISM: 281


"...in Tanzania the only true justification for secondary education is that it is needed by the few for service to the many."

FREEDOM AND SOCIALISM: 281


"There must be the same kind of relationship between pupils and teachers within the school community as there is between children and parents in the village."

FREEDOM AND SOCIALISM: 282

"The object of teaching must be the provision of knowledge, skills and attitudes which will serve the student when she or he lives and works in a developing and changing socialist state..."

FREEDOM AND SOCIALISM: 282

"The assumption that teachers are not powerful is one of the biggest fallacies of our society. For teachers can make or ruin our society."

THE POWER OF TEACHERS: 27/8/1966

"It is they, the teachers now at work and now going through training college, who are shaping what Tanzania will become much more than we who do pass laws, make rules, and make speeches."

THE POWER OF TEACHERS: 27/8/1966

"Conversely, a bright teacher who works with enthusiasm – and with the pupils – who encourages the children to help each other, who explains why he is doing certain things and why certain rules exist, that teacher will be forming quite different and very much more constructive attitudes in the minds of his pupils."

THE POWER OF TEACHERS: 27/8/1966

"Our values in life were developed when we were young; the way we regard our fellows, the way we react to the right and wrong – all these things have developed from our childhood experiences at home and at school."

THE POWER OF TEACHERS: 27/8/1966

"The teacher's power is the power to decide whether 'Service' or 'Self'" shall be the dominant motive in Tanzania of 1990 and thereafter."

THE POWER OF TEACHERS: 27/8/1966

"And the truth is that it is teachers more than any other single group of people who determine the attitudes, and who shape the ideas and aspirations of the nation."

THE POWER OF TEACHERS: 27/8/1966

"It does not matter what the teacher says in Civics Classes or elsewhere; they will learn from what he does."

THE POWER OF TEACHERS: 27/8/1966

"But we are what we are in large part because of the attitudes and the ideas we absorbed from our teachers."

THE POWER OF TEACHERS: 27/8/1966

"But the man who treats everyone with respect, who discusses his position clearly, rationally, and courteously with everyone whatever their position that teacher is inculcating a spirit of equality, of friendship, and of mutual respect. And he is teaching by being – which is the most effective teaching technique existing."

THE POWER OF TEACHERS: 27/8/1966

"The real basis of a society of free individuals is the attitude of mind of the individuals who form the free society. And every knowledgeable person now agrees that 'attitudes of mind' are shaped very largely when a person is very young."

THE POWER OF TEACHERS: 27/8/1966

'The fact is, therefore, that those who have the responsibility to work with the young 'have a POWER which is second to none in relation to the future of our society'. That power is shared by two groups– parents and teachers."

THE POWER OF TEACHERS: 27/8/1966

"When a teacher comes into a class tired, or looking tired, dispirited and without any enthusiasm for work, when the teacher demands that every bit of physical labour is done by the children while he watches, or when the teacher acts as if every pupil were a nuisance, a dullard; in such cases the children will develop the idea that work is something to be avoided, that learning is simply something which one gets through, and that the way to use authority is to get other people to work for you."

THE POWER OF TEACHERS: 27/8/1966

"From our traditional African Society we inherit concepts of equality, democracy, and socialism as well as economic backwardness. From the colonial period we inherit concepts of arrogant individualism and competition as well as knowledge about technical progress. It is our teachers who have the real power to determine whether Tanzania will succeed in modernizing the economy without losing the attitudes which allowed every human being to maintain his self–respect, and earn the respect of his fellows while working in harmony with them."

THE POWER OF TEACHERS: 27/8/1966

"We have the philosophy, we have our PLAN, we have our leaders and we have youth on whom the future of our country depends. As the formation of our youth depends for a great deal on their teachers, it is the teachers on whom the success of the Revolution by re–direction depends. Tanzania now has to educate the leaders of tomorrow. Here again we need people trained in Africa and who believe in Africa."

THE POWER OF TEACHERS: 27/8/1966

# 4

# ON FOREIGN RELATIONS

## SECTION A: ON AFRICAN UNITY

"As long as one community has a monopoly of political power and uses that power... to prevent the other communities from having any share in political power... as a solution of racial conflictit is hypocritical and stupid."

FREEDOM AND UNITY: 24

"If the Africans of Africa unite imperialism must go."

FREEDOM AND UNITY: 62

"The balkanization of Africa is a source of weakness to our continent."

FREEDOM AND UNITY: 90

"It is the apostles of *'bado kidogo'* (when they really mean 'never') and the apostles of balkanization whom we must ask to produce their membership cards in the imperialistic clubs... If we want to look for stooges and tribalists we must look into the camp of the bados."

FREEDOM AND UNITY: 93

"Only with unity can we be sure that Africa really governs Africa."

FREEDOM AND UNITY: 190

"We must use the African national states as an instrument for the reunification of Africa, and not allow our enemies to use them as tools for dividing Africa."

FREEDOM AND UNITY: 194

"On each occasion that we attack each other those who wish to control us for their own purposes jump for joy."

**FREEDOM AND UNITY: 206**

"There is not going to be a god who will bring about African Unity by merely willing unity and saying, 'Let there be unity.'"

**FREEDOM AND UNITY: 216**

"...different African states are in danger of being involved on opposite sides in quarrels which do not concern them. If there were real African unity, moral blackmail would impossible."

**FREEDOM AND UNITY: 213 WAPI**

"One of the hard facts we have to face on our way to African Unity is that this Unity means – on the part of countries – the surrender of sovereignty, and – on the part of individual leaders – the surrender of high position. We must face quite squarely the fact that so far there has been no such surrender in the name of African Unity."

**FREEDOM AND UNITY: 253**

"The world's past is the era of nationalism, and because it is our past it is also the present. Our educational systems have led to the development of exclusive national loyalties, and to concepts of national pride and superiority. They are still doing so. These are the values of the vast mass of the world's citizens."

FREEDOM AND UNITY: 283

"I am becoming increasingly convinced that we are divided between those who genuinely want a continental government and will patiently work for its realization, removing the obstacles, one by one; and those who simply use a phrase 'Union Government' for the purpose of propaganda. Nothing could be more calculated to bring ridicule to the whole concept of a continental government in Africa than this incessant and oft-repeated propaganda."

FREEDOM AND UNITY: 300-301

"Psychologically we have been so successful that no African leader, even if he did not believe in such unity, would dare say so. What is needed, therefore, is not more preaching about unity, but more practicing of unity."

FREEDOM AND UNITY: 300

"But the 'Union Government' we are told, does not require the surrender of sovereignty at all by the individual states. It is some curious animal to which our individual states do not surrender sovereignty, and yet somehow becomes the strong instrument which we require to fulfill the purposes of modern states."

FREEDOM AND UNITY: 301

"The curious argument is advanced that the more balkanized we remain the better for the achievement of a Union Government."

FREEDOM AND UNITY: 301

"Thirty-six separate sticks of wood might each break under the weight of a heavy burden; but what if those thirty-six sticks of wood are bound together? Then the burden can be carried safely, and every single stick remain whole."

FREEDOM AND UNITY: 326

"Africa must travel together, as one, or no part of it will arrive at its destination."

FREEDOM AND UNITY: 327

"Africa is a number of independent sovereign states each one of which is subject to almost unbearable pressures. And the greatest threat to any of us is the existence of the other independent African states."

FREEDOM AND UNITY: 336

"For each one of us is so weak in isolation that we compete with each other for the favour of the wealthy, and our separate but contiguous economies strain and weaken each other as they move in different directions at the same time."

FREEDOM AND UNITY: 336

"Again, each of the African states is separately so weak in relation to the outside world, and so dependent on it, that hardly any decisions can be made without a consideration of the attitudes which larger powers may consequently adopt. For any African country to take any step which might arouse hostility from a major power is an act of great courage, and often of self–sacrifice."

FREEDOM AND UNITY: 337

"The twentieth century is littered with the wrecks of Federations which have failed because they were not based on the will of the people involved, or because they were not strong enough to stand against the prevailing winds of international politics and economics."

FREEDOM AND UNITY: 349

"The man whose contribution merits a footnote in the history of the United Africa will deserve more of the future, than he whose obstinacy, fear or pride, prevents or delays the day when that history can be written."

FREEDOM AND UNITY: 350

"Tanzania is not yet wholly free; because Africa is not wholly free."

FREEDOM AND SOCIALISM: 34

"...every extra road, railway or telephone line, means that Africa is pulled closer together."

FREEDOM AND SOCIALISM: 208

"Can African Unity be built on this foundation of existing and growing nationalism?"

FREEDOM AND SOCIALISM: 208

"...the present organization of Africa into nation states means inevitably that Africa drifts apart unless definite and deliberate counteracting steps are taken."

FREEDOM AND SOCIALISM: 210

"And the truth is that as each of us develops his own state we raise more and more barriers between ourselves."

FREEDOM AND SOCIALISM: 211

"For while it is certainly true that in the long run the whole of Africa, and all its peoples, would be best served by unity, it is equally true, as Lord Keynes is reported to have said, that 'in the long run we are all dead.'"

FREEDOM AND SOCIALISM: 211

"Everything will be done and said which can sow suspicion and disunity between us until finally our people, and our leaders, say—let us carry on alone, let us forget this mirage of unity and freedom for the whole of Africa.' And then, in 150 years' time, Africa will be where Latin America is now, instead of having the strength and economic well–being which is enjoyed by the United States of America."

FREEDOM AND SOCIALISM: 211

"To talk of unity as though it would be panacea of all ills, is to walk naked into a den of hungry lions."

FREEDOM AND SOCIALISM: 212

"It is not impossible to achieve African Unity through nationalism, just as it was not impossible for various tribal associations or tribally-based parties to merge themselves into one nationalist movement."

FREEDOM AND SOCIALISM: 212

"The African nations, and particularly the African leaders, must be loyal to each other."

FREEDOM AND SOCIALISM: 212

"I do not imagine that all my Regional Commissioners in Tanzania like and admire each other – I hope they do, but I would not guarantee it! But, however much they may argue in private, they do not attack each other in public."

FREEDOM AND SOCIALISM: 213

"For African Unity does not have to be a dream; it can be a vision which inspires us. Whether that is so, depends upon us."

FREEDOM AND SOCIALISM: 216

"The weakness of Africa is a constant invitation and a constant encouragement to the exploiters of Africa to suck Africa with impunity."

FREEDOM AND SOCIALISM: 219

"...the truth is that every part of Africa needs Africa as a whole, and Africa as a whole needs every small part of the continent."

FREEDOM AND SOCIALISM: 218

"We cannot move ourselves to the moon in order to get away from our neighbours! We have therefore to live together, and somehow we have to find a way of living together."

FREEDOM AND SOCIALISM: 220

"Africa is not really as weak in relation to the rest of the world as it sometimes appears. It is weak only while our different states allow themselves to be separated from one another."

FREEDOM AND SOCIALISM: 221

"Our national divisions must therefore be taken for what they are – means of administration. We must not allow them to divide Africa."

FREEDOM AND SOCIALISM: 222

"But the willingness of Africa to be divided, and the failure of Africa to honour her own resolutions on different subjects, these things are damaging Africa now, and threatening our whole future."

FREEDOM AND SOCIALISM: 222

"Our interests are ignored, our opinions are brushed aside and our warnings disregarded. And this happens because the states of Africa are disunited – for no other reason than that."

FREEDOM AND SOCIALISM: 291

"For they see 38 different states, which are tied together by the facts of geography and by mutual need, ignore their joint potential in the hopeless chase after the mirage of individual greatness."

FREEDOM AND SOCIALISM: 291

"African unity is not lost. It will never be lost while there are people conscious of the need for it, and willing to work for it."

FREEDOM AND SOCIALISM: 292

"We have to accept our differences, and accommodate them. There is no other way."

FREEDOM AND SOCIALISM: 294

"Our brothers may be wrong, but they remain our brothers. This appears to me the only attitude open to us on our path to real unity."

FREEDOM AND SOCIALISM: 297

"For the O.A.U. is a geographical not an ideological, grouping."

FREEDOM AND SOCIALISM: 297

"A man who has been sick for years may well overestimate his strength when he first gets on his feet, so that he falls and hurts himself... to the life of a bedridden invalid. He rests a while, and then tries again– more slowly and carefully at the beginning. He learns from his mistakes. Africa must do likewise."

FREEDOM AND SOCIALISM: 298-299

"The true revolutionary in Africa has to do two things at one and the same time... he must keep the goal clearly in his sights... He must, in other words, be a realistic idealist! I should add that I do not myself believe this is a contradiction in terms!"

FREEDOM AND SOCIALISM: 299

"Differences of economic and political organization can certainly be accommodated within the arrangements for East African cooperation..."

FREEDOM AND SOCIALISM: 378

## SECTION B: NON-ALIGNMENT

"...it can be stated quite categorically that no part of Africa will ever become a duplicate copy of any part of Europe."

FREEDOM AND UNITY: 116

"...we shall be working out a new synthesis, a way of life that draws from Europe as well as Africa, from Islam as well as Christianity, from communalism and individualism."

FREEDOM AND UNITY: 116

"Africa's vital contribution to the world at this stage of history must be to welcome new ideas freely and openly, and then to use them."

FREEDOM AND UNITY: 122

"One of the greatest dangers facing us in Africa is the temptation to stop thinking about an idea because the label 'imperialist' or 'Communist' has been attached to it."

FREEDOM AND UNITY: 122

"...the success or otherwise of this Second Scramble depends on us; on whether we allow ourselves to become dupes of other people – or of the slogans we used in our struggle for freedom from colonialism."

FREEDOM AND UNITY: 205–206

"Two major power blocs now exist, neither of which can destroy the other without itself being destroyed, and both of which are for the present powerful enough to prevent other nations expanding to challenge them in importance."

FREEDOM AND UNITY: 271

"This is what independence means – not the right to a flag, or a seat at the United Nations, but the right to determine our own policies in the light of the interests of the United Republic, and of Africa, and of world peace."

FREEDOM AND UNITY: 314

"But we did not struggle for our independence in order to sell it to the highest bidder. Our internal affairs, and our international stand on world issues must both be determined by us."

FREEDOM AND UNITY: 314

"Not even for the sake of our national security or our economic development can we allow our nation to succumb to outside control – direct or indirect."

FREEDOM AND UNITY: 314

"We have no enemies, and we do not want them. And we are not prepared to let other people fight their enemies in our country."

FREEDOM AND UNITY: 314

"Do not let us imagine that this will be easy. The world is divided into various conflicting groups, and each one of these groups is anxious for allies in Africa, and even more anxious that its opponent shall not find friends."

FREEDOM AND UNITY: 314

"We wish to be friendly with all and we will never allow our friends to choose our enemies for us."

FREEDOM AND UNITY: 323-324

"...we have a saying in East Africa; when elephants fight it is the grass which gets crushed. We have therefore determined to adopt a policy of non – alignment in relation to international conflicts which do not concern us. Where there are hostile blocs facing each other on the world stage Tanzania will ignore the threats or blandishments from both sides, and pursue her own interests."

FREEDOM AND UNITY: 323

"We shall see for ourselves what are China's intentions towards us. We shall not be told by others."

FREEDOM AND UNITY: 324

"...'non–alignment'... It really means trying to be friends with all and not quarrelling with one half of the world in order to seek a security with the other half."

FREEDOM AND UNITY: 329

"It is not intelligent to reject an accolade from the West on democracy in order to seek one from the East on socialism."

FREEDOM AND SOCIALISM: 20

"Tanzania does not need a certificate of approval about its internal policies from any outside group. The only approval our policies need is the approval of the Tanzanian people."

FREEDOM AND SOCIALISM: 21

"Frankly I find this anxiety about the health of Tanzania sometimes funny, sometimes irritating, and always odd."

FREEDOM AND SOCIALISM: 51

"...Africans are not European, could not become European, and do not want to become European. They demand instead the right to be Africans in Africa, and to determine their own cultural, economic, and political future."

FREEDOM AND SOCIALISM: 145

"We have declared that we wish to build our economy on the basis of the equality of all citizens, and have specifically rejected the concept of creating a class system where one group of people owns the means of production for the purpose of getting personal profit and another group works for them."

FREEDOM AND SOCIALISM: 192

"They have not yet accustomed themselves to the idea that we are independent, and that our friendship will now be genuine but our decisions will be our own."

FREEDOM AND SOCIALISM: 193

"If we are to rely upon one of the contending power blocs and be hostile to the other, then we must determine all our policies according to the interests of that bloc, and not according to the special interests of Tanzania."

FREEDOM AND SOCIALISM: 193

"Tanzanians are sufficiently interested to develop Tanzania in the interests of Tanzania, and only Tanzanians can say what these interests are."

UNIVERSITY LECTURE 5/8/1967

## SECTION C: THE UNITED NATIONS

"We cannot, unlike other countries, send rockets to the moon, but we can send rockets of love and hope to all our fellow men wherever they may be..."

FREEDOM AND UNITY: 72

"We have indeed achieved a 'balance of terror' in the world which effectively prevents the establishment of a system of world law by force. The only way in which this can now be achieved is therefore by agreement between the contending powers."

FREEDOM AND UNITY: 271-272

"At any level, however, there is only one way in which law can be made by agreement. And there is only one way in which disputes can be settled peacefully when there is no law. That is by talking until agreement is reached."

FREEDOM AND UNITY: 272

"While people are talking they are not fighting and they may find a compromise which saves them from this disaster."

FREEDOM AND UNITY: 273

"Further, it is possible to use talk to obstruct, as well as to seek a settlement."
FREEDOM AND UNITY: 274

"For agreement on any dispute always involved compromise, and the adjustment of plans."
FREEDOM AND UNITY: 274

"The danger to peace comes when failure to agree at a particular time leads to action other than mere talking, for example, when having disagreed, the contestants send troops into an area about which there is a boundary dispute."
FREEDOM AND UNITY: 274

"Yet for conflicting countries to lose the one place where they sit down together would be to say that their particular dispute cannot be settled by argument, and must be settled by extermination."
FREEDOM AND UNITY: 276

"The fact is that we all have to live together; a country does not cease to exist as an international entity because other states have disputes with it."
FREEDOM AND UNITY: 276

"For there is nothing more obvious in the modern world than the fact that it is easier, from a political point of view, to fight than to talk."

FREEDOM AND UNITY: 283

"The real enemy in the modern world is, in fact, the man who refuses to talk about the disputes in which he is involved."

FREEDOM AND UNITY: 284

"The challenge of the twentieth century is the conversion of nationalism into internationalism. Our success depends on whether we have the courage to place our trust in world institutions of which we are such a small part, and whether the leaders of nation states will lead in the direction of unity on the basis of equality."

FREEDOM AND UNITY: 284

"I entirely agree that unless unity is achieved within a reasonable time after independence it will become increasingly more difficult to attain."

FREEDOM AND UNITY: 295

"...nations should only enter into a Federation when they can do so with a whole-hearted and unqualified commitment to it."

FREEDOM AND UNITY: 296

"...our foreign policy would be based on the principles of non-alignment... We wanted to be friends with all nations on the basis of national equality and sovereignty, and of mutual respect."

FREEDOM AND SOCIALISM: 51

"We desire friendship with these non-Western nations as well as with Western states, and on the same basis of mutual non-interference with internal affairs."

FREEDOM AND SOCIALISM: 369

"The USA must recover from the delirium of power, and return to the principles upon which her nation was founded."

FREEDOM AND SOCIALISM: 371

"The United Nations is weak when powerful states wish to ignore it. Its servants can only act when the sovereign and independent member nations agree that they shall do so..."

FREEDOM AND SOCIALISM: 51

"Africa has 38 Representatives in the General Assembly of the United Nations; a good part of the time we divide our votes and cancel each other out. The rest of the time we form a bloc which might determine whether a resolution is passed or not. But having passed it we are too weak, or too divided, to see that it is implemented."

FREEDOM AND DEVELOPMENT 16-17

" ...discussions our representatives hold in the United Nations; all these things help to avoid a public display of disunity and help to prevent the kind of inter-African suspicions which others can use to drive a wedge between us."

FREEDOM AND DEVELOPMENT 20

"...the United Nations has failed to take any effective steps to dislodge this... tyranny from South–West Africa."

FREEDOM AND DEVELOPMENT 113

"At the United Nations and at other international conference, the voice of Sweden – and of other Scandinavian countries – is heard in support of humanity and justice. Your people... help to remind us that this struggle is one for humanity and is not just a matter of colour."

FREEDOM AND DEVELOPMENT 335–336

# 5

# ON TANZANIAN REVOLUTION

## SECTION A: REVOLUTION

"In Africa now the social ethic is changing, and has to change, from one appropriate to a tribal society to one appropriate to a national society."

FREEDOM AND UNITY: 20

"And these changes must be positive, they must be initiated and shaped by Africa and not simply be a reaction to events which affect Africa."

FREEDOM AND UNITY: 22

"...the choice is not between change or no change, the choice for Africa is between changing or being changed."

FREEDOM AND UNITY: 22

"We know that some human dislocation is inevitable in this process but we believe that much more would ultimately be involved in doing nothing."

FREEDOM AND UNITY: 22

"...our most critical years are going to be the first years of independence."

FREEDOM AND UNITY: 73

"Society, like everything else, must either move or stagnate and and in stagnation lies death."

FREEDOM AND UNITY: 120

"From now on we are fighting not man but nature, and we are seeking to wrest from nature a better and fuller life for ourselves."

FREEDOM AND UNITY: 139

"The Tanganyika we have inherited is a very different Tanganyika from the one we are setting out to build and to bequeath to our children."

FREEDOM AND UNITY: 181

"...the conditions in which many of the people now live and move are a negation of human dignity, and a disgrace to the twentieth-century world."

FREEDOM AND UNITY: 232

"...discontent is only 'divine' if it can lead to a transformation of the situation."

FREEDOM AND UNITY: 235

"Indeed one of the distinguishing characteristics of an underdeveloped country is the low productivity of its workers and land."

FREEDOM AND UNITY: 235

"In Tanganyika it is not much help producing a scheme which requires an army of skilled or educated agriculture workers, because we do not have them now, and despite all our efforts will not have them for many years to come."

FREEDOM AND UNITY: 238

"The world renowned expert is often an embarrassment to us."

FREEDOM AND UNITY: 242

"I know that the people of this country have the necessary capacity to overcome disappointments and convert them into triumphs. Our internal experience demonstrates this."

FREEDOM AND UNITY: 254

"We have no oil or other raw material for which the rest of the world is crying out. Our only resources are the land and the people, and it is through the organized exploitation of these two that we shall have to make progress."

FREEDOM AND UNITY: 307

"A revolution in under-developed countries like the United Republic means an economic revolution if it is to mean anything."

FREEDOM AND UNITY: 308

"If our farmers are ignorant, conservative, and backward, then our nation will be ignorant, conservative, and backward. Unless our farmers have the knowledge and attitudes which encourage progress to a better life, then all the fine buildings of the towns, the good roads, and everything else, will be like the handful of fresh fish with which a dishonest salesman tries to cover up the smell of the rotten fish underneath..."

FREEDOM AND UNITY: 316

"...peace and human justice are inter-linked and should be inter-linked."

FREEDOM AND DEVELOPMENT: 2

"Freedom won for a people by outsiders is lost to those outsiders, however good their intentions, or however much the outsiders had desired to free their oppressed brothers."

FREEDOM AND DEVELOPMENT: 3

"No nation has the right to make decisions for another nation; no people for another people."
FREEDOM AND DEVELOPMENT: 3

"It is important therefore to realize that the policy of *'Ujamaa Vijijini'* is not intended to be merely a revival of settlement schemes under another name."
NOT FOUNDFREEDOM AND DEVELOPMENT: 7

"...an *ujamaa* village must be governed by members themselves, equally."
FREEDOM AND DEVELOPMENT: 8

"Until Africa is one economic unit, it will remain the plaything of the great powers of the world; and the only way for a people to keep control of one economic unit is to have one representative political power covering the whole area."
FREEDOM AND DEVELOPMENT: 17

"Our country is bedeviled by its present poverty; people are sick, ignorant, and live in very poor conditions, because we do not produce enough wealth to be able to eradicate these evils."
FREEDOM AND SOCIALISM: 9

"Socialism does not spring ready-made out of the womb of violence."

FREEDOM AND SOCIALISM: 23

"...a violent revolution was a necessary pre-condition for the establishment of an opportunity to begin the work of building socialism, the early period of transition towards this goal will have certain kinds of non-socialist characheristics."

FREEDOM AND SOCIALISM: 24

"We in Tanzania certainly have a very long way to go before we shall begin to be satisfied with our achievement."

FREEDOM AND SOCIALISM: 135

"...nothing has a perfect beginning; time is required for anything to be perfect."

FREEDOM AND SOCIALISM: 136

"...our real security and freedom does not depend on large national armies. It depends on economic progress, on our unity in Africa, and on our united diplomacy."

FREEDOM AND SOCIALISM: 221

"We have been oppressed a great deal, we have been exploited a great deal and we have been disregarded a great deal. It is our weakness that has led to our being oppressed, exploited and disregarded. Now we want a revolution – a revolution which brings to an end our weakness, so that we are never again exploited, oppressed, or humiliated."

FREEDOM AND SOCIALISM: 235

"The mistake we are making is to think that development begins with industries. It is a mistake because we do not have the means to establish many modern industries in our country."

FREEDOM AND SOCIALISM: 241

"Tarmac roads, too, are mostly found in towns and are of special value to the motor-car owners. Yet if we have built those roads with loans, it is again the farmer who produces the goods which will pay for them."

FREEDOM AND SOCIALISM: 243

"If we are not careful we might get to the position where the real exploitation in Tanzania is that of the town dwellers exploiting the peasants."

FREEDOM AND SOCIALISM: 243

"Everybody wants development; but not everybody understands and accepts the basic requirements for development. The biggest requirement is hard work."

FREEDOM AND SOCIALISM: 244

"But the men who live in villages (and some of the women in town) are on leave for half of their life."

FREEDOM AND SOCIALISM: 245

"Women who live in the villages work harder than anybody else in Tanzania."

FREEDOM AND SOCIALISM: 245

"The energies of the millions of men in the villages and thousands of women in the towns which are at present wasted in gossip, dancing and drinking are a great treasure which could contribute more towards the development of our country than anything we could get from rich nations."

FREEDOM AND SOCIALISM: 245

"...it would be more appropriate for us to spend time in the villages showing the people how to bring about development through their own efforts rather than going on so many long and expensive journeys abroad in search of development money."

FREEDOM AND SOCIALISM: 246

"In our country work should be something to be proud of, and laziness, drunkenness and idleness should be things to be ashamed of."

FREEDOM AND SOCIALISM: 247

"What we do have is land in abundance and people who are willing to work hard for their own improvement. It is the use of these latter resources which will decide whether we reach our total goals or not. If we use these resources in a spirit of self–reliance as the basis for development, then we shall make progress slowly but surely."

FREEDOM AND SOCIALISM: 272

"...it would be grossly unrealistic to imagine that in the near future more than a small proportion of our people will live in towns and work in modern industrial enterprises."

FREEDOM AND SOCIALISM: 273

"It is therefore the villages which must be made into places where people live a good life; it is in the rural areas that people must be able to find their material well–being and their satisfactions."

FREEDOM AND SOCIALISM: 273

"It is possible, as we have found out in Tanzania, for farmers to be exploited even by their own co-operative and their own state if the machinery is not correct, or if the managers and workers are inefficient and dishonest. And it is possible for group ownership to result in a stultification of development, and such stagnation, that in the end the producers would get greater benefit from controlled forms of individual exploitation."

FREEDOM AND SOCIALISM: 306

"Socialism cannot be imposed upon people; they can be guided; they can be led. But ultimately they must be involved."

FREEDOM AND SOCIALISM: 309

"The *'jembe'* will have to be eliminated by the plough before the latter can be eliminated by the tractor."

UNIVERSITY LECTURE: 05/08/1967

"The Arusha Declaration lays down a policy of revolution by evolution; we shall become a socialist, self–reliant society through our growth."

UNIVERSITY LECTURE: 05/08/1967

"To be realistic, therefore, we must stop dreaming of developing Tanzania through the establishment of large, modern industries."

UNIVERSITY LECTURE: 05/08/1967

## SECTION B: RURAL DEVELOPMENT

"Only by creating and developing our own exclusive organization could we begin to develop confidence in our own abilities or in the Tanganyika of that time..."

FREEDOM AND UNITY: 3

"We called for equality; our people now demand that their leaders accord it to everyone regardless of his economic or social degree."

FREEDOM AND UNITY: 4

"The principles of individual freedom and the rule of law require that no person is arrested and held without quickly being convicted of illegal actions."

FREEDOM AND UNITY: 6

"The traditional order is dying; the question which has yet to be answered is what will be built on our past and, in consequence, what kind of society will eventually replace the traditional one."

FREEDOM AND UNITY: 6

"Man's existence in society involves an evitable and inescapable conflict– a conflict of his own desires... freedom to pursue his own interests and his own inclinations."

FREEDOM AND UNITY: 7

"In the case of family property each individual has a right; in case of the private property, there may be an expectation but there is no automatic right."

FREEDOM AND UNITY: 10

"But the obligation to work is a recognized part of society, as unquestioned as the right of sharing."

FREEDOM AND UNITY: 11

"...the fact that murders continue in every society; does not prevent every society trying to eliminate them, to reduce their causes and discourage the expression of man's violent instincts."

FREEDOM AND UNITY: 16

"It is essential that our concept of society is adapted to the present day; only then will any of our present social groupings really be free to pursue their own policies."

FREEDOM AND UNITY: 19


"...we can create greater African unity by unions, federations or mergers of the present nation states, so that the number of sovereign societies in Africa is reduced."

FREEDOM AND UNITY: 20


"The race quarrel is a stupid quarrel, it can be a very tragic quarrel."

FREEDOM AND UNITY: 29


"Emphasis by the Government should not have been on the reduction of cattle, but on converting this form of capital, which is destructive to the land, into another form of capital, which can still give the Sukuma more wealth but which is not destructive to land."

FREEDOM AND UNITY: 39

"I would feel that I am cheating the people and cheating my own organization if I remained on the Council, receiving allowances and attending sundowners as an Honorable Member giving the impression that I was still of some service on that Council, when in fact I know that I am useless."

FREEDOM AND UNITY: 52

"What is the origin of the right to possess wealth?... This right originates from only one factor; the fact that man is nobody's property. He owns himself... whenever he uses his intellect, his health and his ability to make anything, that thing becomes his property..."

FREEDOM AND UNITY: 53

"If we allow land to be sold like a robe, within a short period there would only be a few Africans possessing land... and all the others would be tenants..."

FREEDOM AND UNITY: 55

"The system of leasehold gives a person all these three things; sufficient land, security and a way of raising capital. What more does a citizen want?"

FREEDOM AND UNITY: 57

"We shall be as clean in our methods as we are in our aims. We shall publicly declare our methods as we publicly declare our aims. We shall not submit to humiliation."

FREEDOM AND UNITY: 59

"Tanzania is not now a socialist country; it is only a country whose people have firmly committed themselves to building socialism."

FREEDOM AND SOCIALISM: 1

"First, and most central of all, is that under socialism Man is the purpose of all social activity. The service of man, the furtherance of his human development is in fact the purpose of society itself."

FREEDOM AND SOCIALISM: 4

"Every member will contribute, by his work, to the total of wealth and welfare produced by the society, and he will receive a return in proportion to his efforts and his contribution to the well-being of the community."

FREEDOM AND SOCIALISM: 5

"...the first priority of production must be the manufacture and the distribution of such goods as will allow every member of the society to have sufficient food, clothing and shelter, to sustain a decent life."

FREEDOM AND SOCIALISM: 11

"A man's relationship with his God is a personal matter for him and him alone; his beliefs about the hereafter are his own affair."

FREEDOM AND SOCIALISM: 12

"Socialism is secular. It has nothing to say about whether there is a God. Certainly it rests on the assumption of the equality of man, but people can reach this conclusion by many routes."

FREEDOM AND SOCIALISM: 13

"There is not the slightest necessity for people to study metaphysics and decide whether there is one God, many Gods, or no God, before they can be socialist."

FREEDOM AND SOCIALISM: 13

"There is no magic formula, and no short cut to socialism. We can only grope our way forward, doing our best to think clearly– and scientifically– about our own conditions in relation to our objectives."

FREEDOM AND SOCIALISM: 19

"The conscious and deliberate frugality with which your people and your Government (China) efficiently and joyfully conduct their affairs was a big lesson..."

FREEDOM AND SOCIALISM: 34

"To burden the farm with very heavy debts at the outset, and at the same time to make it appear that Government can provide all services, is not the best way of promoting activity."

FREEDOM AND SOCIALISM: 44

"...the donor countries can be, and will be, selective in the projects they agree to help, and even in the countries they agree to help."

FREEDOM AND SOCIALISM: 46


"Our watchword must be 'frugality'. This must run through the whole expenditure of Government."

FREEDOM AND SOCIALISM: 49


"...if we want socialism and aim at developing our country on the basis of socialist principles, it is because we believe that socialism is good."

FREEDOM AND SOCIALISM: 137


"A person who serves himself is a true master. He has no worries, he has confidence in himself and is confident of his own actions."

FREEDOM AND SOCIALISM: 139


"You are selected to lead your fellow men, it does not mean that you are more intelligent than they are – especially the elders."

FREEDOM AND SOCIALISM: 146

"Socialism means that no person uses his wealth to exploit others."

FREEDOM AND SOCIALISM: 142

"...no man can expect help from his colleagues if he is not willing to help them. It is even true that in order to eat, a man must be willing to work."

FREEDOM AND SOCIALISM: 142

"Government cannot do anything about the weather, and unfortunately neither can it control world prices– although we continue to work for an international system of price stabilization for primary commodities."

FREEDOM AND SOCIALISM: 158

"When a farmer sells his crop he finds that a whole list of organizations are taking a cut from his money... There are deductions for research, for education, for local government... Services have to be paid for. But there is some evidence to support the view that in the past... the local crop may have been too easily and light heartedly adopted... correcting it is the responsibility of the people..."

FREEDOM AND SOCIALISM: 164

"Let our motto... be 'self–reliance', and in that spirit let us pursue our goal of economic betterment for our country and all its people."
FREEDOM AND SOCIALISM: 174

"...the purpose of establishing the university is to make it possible for us to change these poverty–stricken lives."
FREEDOM AND SOCIALISM: 184

"The role of a university in a developing country is to contribute; to give ideas, manpower, and service for the furtherance of human equality, human dignity, and human development."
FREEDOM AND SOCIALISM: 186

"Peace everywhere is now something which matters to us all; our own human happiness, and our own economic and social progress are involved in it."
FREEDOM AND DEVELOPMENT P. 1

"Education for Self Reliance... it directs the people along the socialist path, but excludes any attempts to whip them into it."
FREEDOM AND DEVELOPMENT P. 3

"The community must own, control, and run
its own activities."

FREEDOM AND DEVELOPMENT P. 6

"My own experience suggests that our
people in the rural areas are prepared to
work together for their common good; in
many places they have never stopped this
traditional custom, and would take quite
easily to an extension of it."

FREEDOM AND DEVELOPMENT P. 6–7

"The selection of the right person as the 'farm
manager' or as the 'farm treasurer' can be
of vital importance; how then can the
members be helped to choose the best man
from among their number?"

FREEDOM AND DEVELOPMENT P. 10

"...African leaders should always refrain from
public displays of disunity. Our quarrels – if
we have any – should be conducted privately!"

FREEDOM AND DEVELOPMENT P. 20

"We have to keep the concept of Africa, as one unit, before our people all the time. In our schools we must teach our children that they are Africans..."

FREEDOM AND DEVELOPMENT P. 19

"Africa today is an exciting place to live in; African development is an exciting challenge, and we have the opportunity to shape and to lead the response to that challenge."

FREEDOM AND DEVELOPMENT P. 24

"There is only one way in which you can cause people to undertake their own development. That is by education and leadership."

FREEDOM AND DEVELOPMENT P. 61

"The people must make the decisions about their own future through democratic procedures. Leadership cannot replace democracy; it must be part of democracy."

FREEDOM AND DEVELOPMENT P. 62

"If we are to live our lives in peace and harmony, and if we are to achieve our ambitions of improving the conditions under which we live, we must have both freedom and discipline."

FREEDOM AND DEVELOPMENT P. 65

"An *Ujamaa* village is a voluntary association of people who decide of their own free will to live together and work together for their common good."

FREEDOM AND DEVELOPMENT P. 67

"The decision to join with others in creating an *Ujamaa* village is an individual one. But once that decision is made, then normal democratic rules will apply to all members."

FREEDOM AND DEVELOPMENT P. 68

"By developing the people of Tanzania, we are developing Tanzania. For Tanzania is the people; and the people means everyone. (*Tanzania ni ya Watanzania; na Watanzania ni wote*). No one person has the right to say, 'I am the people.'"

FREEDOM AND DEVELOPMENT P. 70

"It is absolutely taboo for a socialist country to divide people according to their colour and afterwards to persecute them because of their colour, even if they are peasants or workers."
FREEDOM AND DEVELOPMENT P. 77

"We have to make choices between good things, not between good things and bad things: to plan means to choose."
FREEDOM AND DEVELOPMENT P. 84

"It is very good to increase our population, because our country is large and there is plenty of unused land. But it is necessary to remember that these 350,000 extra people every year will be babies in arms, not workers."
FREEDOM AND DEVELOPMENT P. 87

"...Tanzania is involved in a world based on technology, and we shall remain backward and dependent upon others until we are able to produce our own people with scientific skills."
FREEDOM AND DEVELOPMENT P. 88

"Our farmers have expanded the acreage they cultivate; they have worked harder. But almost everywhere they are still using the hoe, *jembe*, and *shoka*. They have not yet changed the tools they work with. The expansion possible with these tools is very limited..."

FREEDOM AND DEVELOPMENT P. 91

"Our present attitude to food is the result of ignorance, indifference and indolence."

FREEDOM AND DEVELOPMENT P. 93

"For the truth is that the people of this country are the real developers of Tanzania, as well as being the purpose of Tanzanian development."

FREEDOM AND DEVELOPMENT P. 103

"Let those who do not create continue to criticize; their contribution to our development is comparable to the contribution to literature of those whose sole activity consists of criticizing other writers."

FREEDOM AND DEVELOPMENT P. 145

"Economic cooperation among ourselves is an essential part of the struggle to maintain our political freedom."
FREEDOM AND DEVELOPMENT P. 171

"And because humanity is in fact one and indivisible, and because freedom is indivisible, it is also an affront to every free man, regardless of colour."
FREEDOM AND DEVELOPMENT P. 211

"We are neither fools nor impractical idealists. But it is one thing to recognize the facts of an inheritance while you work to change that pattern."
FREEDOM AND DEVELOPMENT P. 211

"...the Church... should be one of the group of nations, and institutions which reject domination by the rich for the benefit of the rich."
FREEDOM AND DEVELOPMENT P. 226

"The trouble is that the newspapers talk about difficulties much more than they talk about successes. Hard, steady work for unity is not exciting – it provides no headlines."
FREEDOM AND DEVELOPMENT P. 240

"...circumstances can be used as our excuse for inaction, or they can be seized and made to work for the objectives which have been decided upon."

FREEDOM AND DEVELOPMENT P. 267

"For the first time in African history, two nations submerged their sovereignty into one, and progress towards unity in Africa was shown to be a matter of political will on the part of the people and their leaders."

FREEDOM AND DEVELOPMENT P. 276

"Although a water point does not have a spectacular appearance, it can often be more important for the progress of the people in the area than an imposing building, or a factory, put somewhere else..."

FREEDOM AND DEVELOPMENT P. 320

"Care is necessary, but a desperate fear of mistakes results only in stagnation."

FREEDOM AND DEVELOPMENT P. 350

## SECTION C: SELF-RELIANCE

"There is nothing good that can be had free of charge."

FREEDOM AND UNITY: 58

"The problems of the underdeveloped countries are thus two-fold. Firstly, to increase production of the goods and services which people need; and secondly, to increase the consumption of the goods and services which denote a good and free life."

FREEDOM AND UNITY: 236

"We soon learn too that our determination to decide for ourselves the pattern of our future society complicates our endeavours to attract capital to our countries."

FREEDOM AND UNITY: 239

"Once you need outside aid it is impossible to avoid decisions with a political content being made outside your own country."

FREEDOM AND UNITY: 239

"By itself the increased production achieves little; stable and assured markets are essential."

FREEDOM AND UNITY: 243

"The 'free international market' is unavoidably, an arena in which the weakest goes to the wall."

FREEDOM AND UNITY: 246

"'Trade not Aid' is our objective, but in the meantime 'Aid' can be invaluable in helping us to reach that goal."

FREEDOM AND UNITY: 250

"A continuation of the present chaos in which the rich get richer and the poor stay poor is unacceptable to those of us who are conscious of our poverty. The only alternative to a world plan is, therefore, an acceptance of our economic inequality, and deliberate isolationism while we build ourselves up."

FREEDOM AND UNITY: 250

"Each underdeveloped country is like a man who desires to build a fleet of ships. First he builds a rowing boat. With this he sweats, carrying people across rivers until he gets enough profit to build a coaster. With the proceeds of coastal trade he builds first one, and later many ocean going ships. If, however, he tries to send his rowing boat into the ocean it will sink, and he will be back where he started. If, when he gets his coaster it does not flee from the storms, that will sink and he will be back at the rowing boat stage. It is only when he has built up his fleet that he sends ships into hurricane areas."

FREEDOM AND UNITY: 251

"The economies of the underdeveloped countries cannot safely venture into the stormy ocean of unplanned international marketing until they are like ocean going craft. They will get to that position more quickly if there is outside aid appropriate to the need of the time. But until then– regardless of whether aid is obtained or not– if the sea cannot be made calmer by international planning, then we must retreat from it while we build economies strong enough to withstand the unpredictable mischances of a 'free market.'"

FREEDOM AND UNITY: 251

"Yet international trade is like a two-way suction pump; it sucks more from the developing countries into the developed countries than it puts into the developing countries from the developed ones. As a result, the gap between the developed and the developing countries of the world is widening, not narrowing."

FREEDOM AND UNITY: 303

"The desire to help the United Republic is our economic struggle– even the desire for friendship with us– these things come second to what the other nation believes to be its own interests."

FREEDOM AND UNITY: 314

"The only nation which has the interests of the United Republic as its first priority is the United Republic."

FREEDOM AND UNITY: 315

"No country owes Tanzania a living; we have to earn it for ourselves. Sentiment will not make people buy our goods if they do not want them; it is our own responsibility to find, and to supply, every possible market."

FREEDOM AND UNITY: 321-322

"...the truth is that the total amount of external capital aid was less than the amount by which our sisal earnings went down because of the fall in international prices."

FREEDOM AND SOCIALISM: 166

"In my experience the one form of foreign aid which is easy to get from big powers is arms and military training!"

FREEDOM AND SOCIALISM: 220

"We have been oppressed a great deal, we have been exploited a great deal and we have been disregarded a great deal. It is our weakness that has led to our being oppressed, exploited and disregarded. Now we want a revolution– a revolution which brings to an end our weakness, so that we are never again exploited, oppressed or humiliated."

FREEDOM AND SOCIALISM: 235

"By our thoughts, words and actions it appears as if we have come to the conclusion that without money we cannot bring about the revolution we are aiming at."

FREEDOM AND SOCIALISM: 235

"But in any case the prosperous nations have not accepted a responsibility to fight world poverty."

FREEDOM AND SOCIALISM: 239

"Independence cannot be real if a nation depends upon gifts and loans from another for its development."

FREEDOM AND SOCIALISM: 239

"Our tools are our hands, our brains, and our spirit. And these will suffice if we have courage, patience, stamina, and vision."

FREEDOM AND SOCIALISM: 300

"For self-reliance is the means by which people develop."

FREEDOM AND DEVELOPMENT: 9

"...the role of a leader is crucial and good leadership will make all the difference to the socialist success and the material success of such a community."

FREEDOM AND DEVELOPMENT: 9

"...without freedom you get no development, and without development you very soon lose your freedom."

FREEDOM AND DEVELOPMENT 58

"The doctrine of self-reliance does not imply isolationism either politically or economically."

UNIVERSITY LECTURE: 5.08.1967

"Few things make me more angry than a refusal to accept and to work with people from other countries whose participation can make the difference between our plans succeeding or failing."

UNIVERSITY LECTURE: 5.08.1967

"But the truth is that it is not possible to accept socialism without self–reliance, or vice versa."

UNIVERSITY LECTURE: 5.08.1967

"It is not being self–reliant to refuse to carry out the direction of a foreign engineer, a foreign doctor, or a foreign manager, it is just being stupid."

UNIVERSITY LECTURE: 5.08.1967